THE WAY OF THE WOLVES

The Enemy's Planned Strike on Your Life

Alisa Hope Wagner

Dedication

This booklet is dedicated to the Christian Conquerors who face battles daily. Nothing will ever separate you from God's love we have been given freely through Jesus Christ.

> "No, in all these things we are more than conquerors through him who loved us. For I am convinced that neither death nor life, neither angels nor demons, neither the present nor the future, nor any powers, neither height nor depth, nor anything else in all creation, will be able to separate us from the love of God that is in Christ Jesus our Lord" (Romans 8.37-39 NIV).

Thank you to my husband, Daniel, for your continued edits, encouragement, support and love. You will always be the love of my life. Also, to Faith Newton for your keen eye and edits.

Table of Contents

Grey Wolf Dream

I had a dream of a young woman running for her life. In every scene of my dream, she was outnumbered and close to death, but somehow supernatural help came in the form of a sacrifice.

In the first scene, I stood and watched this woman and her friends unknowingly standing in the way of a herd of large bison charging straight at them. Right when the bison were about to smash into the woman's group, a flock of birds supernaturally flew in front of the herd taking the brunt of the impact. The friends scattered and ran.

In the final scene of my dream, the young woman was tired, alone and lost. She had been on the run for many scenes, barely making it out with her life each time. She got only one small reprieve to shower in an empty apartment before heading back outside. She couldn't stay in the apartment

7

because the sinister occupant would be home soon. As I waited for her to get out of the shower, I willed her to hurry up and leave that place.

When she was back in the wilderness, a large, grey wolf came out of the shadows. He was aggressive, mean and evil; and he gave a menacing growl and forcefully attacked her instantly. He tore apart the woman's left foot, and she hurriedly tried to limp away. But I knew she was no match for the wolf's strength and rage. She was injured and could no longer run fast. The wolf approached her ready to strike, and I held my breath to prepare for his attack.

Suddenly, a trio of sleek, golden-brown dachshunds came out of the forest sprinting in unison at lightning speed. They ran right in between the woman and the wolf. The wolf was distracted and attacked one of the dogs, badly wounding him. The woman then limped to the right, and the injured dachshund hobbled to the left.

As I watched, I realized the injured woman now had a chance to survive because of the sacrifice of the hurt dachshund. The wolf turned to the wounded dog and devoured him, giving the woman just enough time to get away.

Then I woke up. My heart was racing. I had never had a dream of a wolf before, and the intense image of him shook me. My dachshund, Rusty, looked just like the ones in my dream, and he is a dearly loved member of our family. I realized that the trio of dachshunds represented the Trinity. And the dachshund who sacrificed itself for the woman was Jesus, the Son of God who saves us all.

> "For God so loved the world that he gave his one and only Son, that whoever believes in him shall not perish but have eternal life" (John 3.16 NIV).

When I looked up what a wolf symbolized, the answer was what I expected: Satan and evil (1). I know that real wolves are part of

God's creation and are equal in beauty and purpose to all creatures, but in this dream, the wolf was symbolic of evil, hatred and a desire to devour. It was the embodiment of Satan.

Jesus Himself used the wolf and the lamb in the parable of the "The Good Shepherd and His Sheep," comparing humans to the lambs and the wolf to the enemy's attack (2).

> "The hired hand is not the shepherd and does not own the sheep. So when he sees the wolf coming, he abandons the sheep and runs away. Then the wolf attacks the flock and scatters it" (John 10.12 NIV).

So in this dream, I know that the wolf represents the one in Jesus' parable who is attacking the flock. This Grey Wolf was Satan, and his evil plan was to strike down the vulnerable, injured young woman. I wondered how many of us in the world experience the planned attacks of Satan and have no idea how to confront him. Life injures us, as it always does, and now Satan has us in his sights. We are wounded and become easy targets because we are hurting and lack understanding, strength and faith.

Therefore, I decided to write this booklet to quickly and powerfully support others with the insights they need to stand their ground and claim victory over the devil's evil plan to destroy their destiny and lives. The Bible says that the devil prowls the earth looking for the injured to devour; however, God has given us this one hope: We resist him by standing firm in faith (3).

> "Resist him, standing firm in the faith, because you know that the family of believers throughout the world is undergoing the same kind of sufferings" (1 Peter 5.9 NIV).

Just like the woman in the dream, we may suffer a little while, but we can trust that God will restore us and make us stronger than before. And when the devil tries to attack us again, we won't run away this time. Instead, we will stand firm, and standing our ground

11

creates the faith we need to claim victory over Satan's planned strike on our lives.

> "And the God of all grace, who called you to his eternal glory in Christ, after you have suffered a little while, will himself restore you and make you strong, firm and steadfast" (1 Peter 5.10 NIV).

In this booklet, I have researched the wolf pack and their highly developed attack plans to devour prey. They are truly amazing beasts, and they will give you insight on how the powers of darkness scheme to take down God's Children. To be certain, an attack is well thought out and orchestrated, and Satan will bide his time until his prey is isolated, exhausted and wounded.

We have only been on this earth a few short years, but Satan and his cohorts have been here since time began. They know what they are doing. Just like the wolf pack, they have a strict hierarchy with a leader and systems of attack. They have learned to communicate well and work together as one evil, powerful pack.

However, there is hope. As Believers, we have Jesus on our side, and He is greater than all the wolf packs that prowl the darkness of the spiritual realm. Do not fear. You are never alone. God is with you, and He will send help via people and resources like this booklet when you feel hurt, alone and defeated.

> "You, dear children, are from God and have overcome them, because the one who is in you is greater than the one who is in the world" (1 John 4.4 NIV).

Plus, we must remember that Jesus too was tempted in every way. Temptations to sin (e.g. fear, worry, lust, covet, hate, etc.) does not mean we have sinned. Satan loves to throw the fiery arrows of temptation our way (Ephesians 6.16). Sometimes, these temptations are so far-fetched that we wonder if our mind is playing tricks on us. Those temptations are not our doing; rather,

13

they are the work of the Grey Wolf. When we are faced with a temptation, we have a choice: we can indulge the temptation to sin or ignore the temptation to sin. Every time we choose to ignore, we become stronger and wiser to the enemy's tactics.

> "For we do not have a high priest who is unable to empathize with our weaknesses, but we have one who has been tempted in every way, just as we are—yet he did not sin" (Hebrews 4.15 NIV).

Keys of Authority

As Believers, Satan and his cohorts have no authority in our lives besides the authority we allow him to take. In the Garden of Eden, God condemned the serpent to slither the ground and eat from the dust of the earth.

> "So the LORD God said to the serpent, 'Because you have done this, Cursed are you above all livestock and all wild animals! You will crawl on your belly and you will eat dust all the days of your life" ([Genesis 3.14 NIV](#)).

This dust is the physical world. Satan, for a short time, is allowed to dwell on this earth and wreak havoc into the physical world from the confines of his dark, spiritual existence. The problem is that we have all been born from the physical world. God made us from the dust of the earth; therefore, Satan has a right through the curse he was given to "crawl" and "eat" dust all the days of his short life on earth.

> "Then the LORD God formed a man from the dust of the ground and breathed into his nostrils the breath of life, and the man became a living being" (Genesis 2.7 NIV).

Yet, we have been given authority through the death and resurrection of Jesus Christ to take back the authority Satan was given. Through the Cross, Jesus took our sins, and He gave us His righteousness (1 Peter 2.24). Now in God's eyes we are blameless and able to have a relationship with Him on this earth which leads into an eternal relationship once our bodies die (Colossians 1.22).

Therefore, although we were born of the earth, we have been given a new birth of the spirit. We are now of both worlds: flesh and the spirit. Flesh was given to us by Adam, and the spirit given to us by Jesus Christ. Which one has more authority? Flesh, which is ruled by Satan or spirit, ruled by the King of

Kings and the Lord of Lords (Revelation 19.16)?

The spirit has more authority because it is of God and is everlasting. Through Christ, we now have the authority over the devil who devours the dust. We may have both flesh and spirit, but the spirit has the ultimate authority, and the flesh must obey. We, in essence, have been given the all-powerful "keys to the kingdom." What we tell to stop, must stop. What we tell to go, must go. Satan has to obey when we declare in accordance to God's will (Mark 11.24 AMP).

> "I will give you the keys of the kingdom of heaven; whatever you bind on earth will be bound in heaven, and whatever you loose on earth will be loosed in heaven" (Matthew 16.19 NIV).

This is good news for us. Yes, we live in a fallen, broken world. And we will suffer and have heartache and feel pain, but as we stand strong in faith, we can resist the planned strike of Satan during times of

17

struggle. Just like in the dream about the wolf and the three dachshunds, God gave us the ultimate sacrifice through His Son Jesus. Out of the three dachshunds, Jesus became the one who took the full weight of Satan's sting, so we can now claim victory over every situation that leads to death and despair.

> "'Where, O death, is your victory? Where, O death, is your sting?' The sting of death is sin, and the power of sin is the law. But thanks be to God! He gives us the victory through our Lord Jesus Christ" (1 Corinthians 15.55-57 NIV).

Now that we know we have the ultimate victory over Satan, we can focus on his tactics by examining the wolf pack, so we can be better prepared to stand strong and defend our ground. When we find ourselves wounded, we don't have to run and hide anymore. In fact, it is in our weakest times that God's grace will shine out all the brighter. So stand firm, weary soul. Help is on the way.

> "But he said to me, 'My grace is sufficient for you, for my power is made perfect in weakness.' Therefore I will boast all the more gladly about my weaknesses, so that Christ's power may rest on me" (2 Corinthians 12.9 NIV).

When we are weak in our strength, we must rely completely on God's strength in us. This is like a young child giving absolute control to his or her parent, trusting that the parent is stronger, smarter and more powerful. Not only that, God is all-loving (1 John 4.16). We can trust God with our lives. We can trust Him with our loved ones. We can trust Him with our destiny. It is good to recognize that we can't achieve God's great purposes alone. Only when we see our weakness, will we finally yield to God's mighty power.

And remember, **Satan can only feed on the dust of the earth or that which is of the flesh**. When we accept Jesus as our Lord and Savior, our flesh dies with Christ on the Cross and is resurrected to new life. Now our spiritual lives have the authority over our

19

physical lives. The proof of this supernatural miracle is that we can now have the Holy Spirit dwelling within us. So whenever we feel like our flesh is getting the best of us, we can envision it dying on the Cross with Christ and resurrecting to new life with spiritual authority.

> "We were therefore buried with him through baptism into death in order that, just as Christ was raised from the dead through the glory of the Father, we too may live a new life" (Romans 6.4 NIV).

If you haven't accepted Jesus as your Lord and Savior, you cannot have lasting authority over the enemy. External parameters that you and others set on you may last for a time, but eventually the flesh will wear down to the constant attacks of the wolf pack. So instead of fighting this fight by yourself in your powerless state, ask Jesus to come into your heart with this simple prayer, so He can fight the battles He has already won for you.

"Jesus, I can't fight these battles on my own. I need you to be Lord over my life, so I can have your forgiveness, power and help. Come into my heart and save me. I want to be reborn in the supernatural, so I can live victoriously now and for eternity. Thank you for forgiving my sins and saving my soul. Now because of Your sacrifice, I can have a relationship with a holy God, and I can live in heaven for eternity. I pray this in Jesus' name, amen."

Wolf Pack's Highway

Our negative thoughts pave a highway for the wolf pack to terrorize our minds, hearts and lives. Since Satan can only feed on dust (what is of the earth, not what is of heaven), every time we have a negative thought of bitterness, guilt, worry, lust, shame, anger, fear, anxiety, discontent, insecurity, etc., the road for these wolves becomes wider and wider until the Grey Wolf and his cohorts have plenty of territory in which to roam.

One negative thought won't incite the enemy's attack, but days, weeks, months and years of the same pattern of negative thoughts will eventually pave a highway of cemented dust. Satan is patient, and he will wait until he has a vantage point. Layers of negative thoughts that have not been rebuked and submitted to God's authority become ground for the Grey Wolf to terrorize us. And just like my dream, he will wait until we are alone, exhausted and wounded before he pounces. So, one way to combat the enemy's attacks before they begin is to not give him room to strike us in the first place. We do this by capturing every negative thought that is not of God and bring it to obedience to Christ.

> "We demolish arguments and every pretension that sets itself up against the knowledge of God, and we take captive every thought to make it obedient to Christ" (2 Corinthians 10.5 NIV).

The Bible says that the tongue (words both thought and spoken) have the power of life and death: "The tongue has the power of life and death, and those who love it will eat its fruit" (Proverbs 18.21 NIV). If we really took this verse seriously, we would be more careful with our words. We should speak only the words we know that are rooted in Christ and pave highways for God to move. Before we can speak words of truth, we first need to identify and capture dust-filled words that we think and speak. Once those are demolished, our minds and hearts will now have capacity to be filled with God's words about us. The following are a few lies:

- I'm so fat.
- I'll never succeed.
- I'm unworthy to be blessed.
- I'm messed up again.
- They'll never love me.
- I'm worthless.
- I wish I were dead.

We may not speak these words out loud, but if we think them over and over again, we are paving a highway for the enemy to attack us. Saying something like, "I'm starving to death," may seem small and culturally acceptable, but it is not suitable in God's kingdom. And if is not of heaven, it will be dust for the wolves to devour. I know this is a small example, but if we truly examine our thoughts and words every day, we will find the reason we aren't living in victory. We will understand why it seems like the wolf pack is constantly nipping at our heels—we have given Satan too much room in our minds and lives!

Once we learn to capture these negatives thoughts and give them to God, we can begin to pave a highway with God's truth found in His Word, the Bible. In order to do this, we need to be in His Word daily. We can't speak words of truth if we don't know them. We can read the Bible, watch sermons, read Christian literature, listen to Christian music, follow Christian blogs, etc. We live in a world where there are so many truth-filled resources, and there is no reason why our minds and hearts shouldn't be brimming with words of truth.

Once we start consuming God's truth, we can not only demolish the dust-paved highways we have built in our minds, we can begin to build truth-paved highways that allow the powerful flow of God in our lives. According to Dr. Caroline Leafe in her book, *Switch on Your Brain*, we can actually replace the old, negative highways of our brain that give Satan access and replace them with new, positive highways that allow the Holy Spirit to fill our lives and situations.

> "As we think, we change the physical nature of our brain. As we consciously direct our thinking, we can wire out toxic patterns of thinking and replace them with healthy thoughts" (5).

Once we capture and rebuke the negative, dust-filled thoughts and words, we can begin to proclaim thoughts and words flowing with truth. This may feel weird at first, especially if negative thinking is our normal, but speaking out truth will begin to pave new pathways in our mind. The more we speak truth, the wider and wider those pathways will become, and they will be roaming ground for God's Spirit in our minds, hearts and lives. The following are words of truth:

- I am healed and full of peace (Isaiah 53.5).

- God has great plans for me (Jeremiah 29.11).

- I am highly favored (Psalm 30.5).

- I am forgiven and redeemed (Ephesians 1.7).

- I am loved by a holy God (Ephesians 2.4-5).

- I am full of worth and value (Matthew 10.29-31).

- I have eternal life with Christ (John 10.27-28).

Do you notice how these declarations can actually be backed by Scripture? The lies of the enemy have absolutely no authority because they cannot be found in God's Word. What we must realize is that a Spirit-filled person is simply a person who has learned to create truth-highways for God to move. A person who lives in defeat and under constant attack is a person who has built dust-paved highways in their minds and lives. But this can end now. We can begin to destroy the enemy's romping ground by capturing every thought. Then we can build highways for God to flow freely within and around us.

We should start now. It may feel like a lot of work at first. Nothing great is built in a day. But the effort will be worth having the fullness of God in our lives. We are children of God, and we want His Spirit to be strong in us. Being under constant attack of the Grey Wolf does not have to be our reality. Let us demolish the wolf pack's playground and make room for God, so we can have all the fruits of His Spirit in our lives.

> "But the fruit of the Spirit is love, joy, peace, forbearance, kindness, goodness, faithfulness, gentleness and self-control. Against such things there is no law" (Galatians 5.22-23 NIV).

Much like a nightmare has residual effects even after we awake; many times we can aggressively stop entertaining the enemy's lies, yet still feel the oppressiveness of them. Instead of getting discouraged, we must realize those feelings will fade as we continue to rebuke them. They are merely the lingering stench of the trash that has already been taken out. We can trust that the odor will eventually diminish as long as we don't bring the trash back in. It takes time, but one day the residual effects of Satan's territory in our minds will be replaced with the fresh aroma of God's presence, and people will take notice.

> "For we are to God the pleasing aroma of Christ among those who are being saved and those who are perishing" (2 Corinthians 2.15 NIV).

Wolf Pack's Tactics

Like stated in the previous chapter, the best way to avoid an attack from the wolves is to not give them ground in the first place. We learn to capture every thought that is not of God and start using our words to create truth-filled highways in our minds for God to move. Instead of harboring these dark thoughts and words, we aggressively expose them, knowing that they are indeed fruitless, destructive and a massive waste of our time (Ephesians 5.11). Then we consume God's Word and other faith-filled resources, so we can begin to produce highways of truth.

Even though we work at exposing and capturing every thought and word, Satan may still find access to our minds and lives. We live in an imperfect world with imperfect people, and life has its hurts, pains and disappointments. Satan is not lazy. Just as God has His Kingdom Plan (Isaiah 46.10-11), the enemy has his work, which is why Jesus

30

Christ came to give us the victory: "…The reason the Son of God appeared was to destroy the devil's work"(1 John 3.8 NIV). The work of the devil vs. the work of Jesus can be seen in one simple, yet profound verse.

> "The thief comes only to steal and kill and destroy; I have come that they may have life, and have it to the full" (John 10.10 NIV).

Now we know what Satan wants to achieve, let us look at his tactics by comparing him and his demons to the wolf pack. Wolves are social animals with a strict hierarchy. They are able to work together to achieve a single goal, which is to bring down their prey. The leader of the pack is the strongest and fiercest of them all, and the rest of the wolves work under his leadership. Therefore, Satan and his cohorts communicate and work as a team when they attack us. We are in essence their prey. And what is their goal? They want to "steal" our power, "kill" our destiny and "destroy" our lives.

31

Wolves are creative animals and will modify their attack patterns based on the situation and prey they are striking, but there are three main methods they almost always use (7).

1. Get their prey on the run.
2. Get their prey full of fear.
3. Get their prey worn down.

First, they try to make the herd flee. Getting the prey on the run and not standing their ground will create fear and havoc, which triggers stumbles and mistakes. It also gives the wolves time to inspect the herd and expose those who are sick, injured and isolated. They will always go after the most vulnerable.

Second, they want to intimidate their prey. Usually, a wolf pack will hunt larger animals, including herds of mule deer, elk and bison (8). These animals could easily trample a wolf; however, if the wolves can nip at the animals' heels enough, growl loud enough and surround their prey, they may be able to intimidate an animal many times their size.

Third, they want to wear down their prey. Wolves can travel for extremely long distances. They have great endurance and will bide their time until their prey loses energy and stamina. Once the animal has lost its strength, it will not be able to put up much of a fight once the wolf pack comes to attack.

What the Grey Wolf is looking for is someone like the woman in my dream. She was isolated, on the run, tired and wounded. Once those four things come into play, she became an easy target to strike.

Satan usually will not strike us when we are strong and full of faith. He knows he's no match for us then. Rather, he remains patient and allows us to create a large enough path for him in our minds that is layered with small pieces of daily negative thoughts. Next, once he knows he has space to roam, he will wait until we are in a season of difficulty. Then, he will begin to nip at us—speaking lie after lie into our lives. Finally, when life hits us with a devastating blow, he strikes. Satan doesn't play fair. When we become wounded, he seizes his prime opportunity to take us down.

We can learn from these three tactics the next time the Grey Wolf and his pack try to strike us. We can overcome every scheme of the enemy if we do the following:

1. Instead of running, we stand firm in faith.

2. Instead of fear, we hang on to courage.

3. Instead of becoming worn down, we renew our strength.

In the next chapter, we will discuss practical ways we can commit to fighting the good fight of faith. Remember, we are in a battle between good and evil, but we are on the victorious side. We have already been given eternal life through Jesus Christ. The battles in this world are fleeting compared to an eternity in heaven with God. Now that we know our victory is guaranteed, let us discover how we can overcome the strike of the enemy.

> "Fight the good fight of the faith. Take hold of the eternal life to which you were called when you made your good confession in the presence of many witnesses" (1 Timothy 6.12 NIV).

Our Fight to Win

Now that we know that the Grey Wolf wants us to FLEE, FEAR and FATIGUE, we can focus on how we can do the complete opposite of what the wolf wants.

First, do not FLEE. Standing firm in faith is easier when we are doing the following three things: Residing in His presence, staying in His Word and remaining in His Church. Remember, the enemy wants us isolated because he knows that when we are alone, we are most vulnerable. However, as we reside in God's presence, He will not only renew our minds (Ephesians 4.23), but He will help us resist the devil (James 4.7). Next, as we stay in God's Word, the Bible becomes alive in our lives and helps us decipher truth from the lies (Hebrews 4.12). Finally, as we remain in church, we receive a unique presence of God that is only found in groups (Matthew 18.20). This is why the Bible directly tells us to keep going to church (Hebrews 10.25). God knows that being part of a "herd" gives us a combined strength and protection we can't have alone.

Second, do not FEAR. Once we have protected ourselves from isolation, we can stand our ground with courage. Standing firm in courage is repeated many times in the Old and New Testaments.

Old Testament:

> "Have I not commanded you? Be strong and courageous. Do not be afraid; do not be discouraged, for the Lord your God will be with you wherever you go" (Joshua 1.9 NIV).

New Testament:

> "Be on your guard; stand firm in the faith; be courageous; be strong" (1 Corinthians 16.13 NIV).

We can take courage because we trust God's provision, protection and purpose. Our courage shows both heaven and earth that we believe that God is greater than all the wolf packs in the world. Jesus has already given us the victory (1 Corinthians 15.57). And Jesus told us Himself that He has given us authority over the power of the enemy (Luke 10.19). As we claim these promises by faith, the Grey Wolf begins to lose his power.

Moreover, God does not give us a timid spirit. Instead, He gives us a spirit of "**power, love and self-discipline**" (2 Timothy 1.7 NIV).

- We have the **power** of the God of the Universe within us. Because of Jesus' Sacrifice on the Cross, the Holy Spirit is our Gift, our Helper and our Guide (John 14.16). We may be weak, but with God we are strong! We can hold onto courage, knowing that God is on our side.

- Also, God's abundant **love** for us disperses all fears (1 John 4.18). When we are full of God's love, there is no room for Satan's fear; and without fear, we can stand firm and keep our courage. We must freely receive God's love, knowing that He loves us so much that He died for us (Romans 5.8). When hanging onto courage, we remind ourselves over and over again how much we are loved.

- Lastly, despite belief to the contrary, we can be **self-disciplined.** Making changes, like demolishing negative thoughts and proclaiming truth-filled thoughts, feels difficult at first. However, after a while a habit will be formed if we don't give up. A habit is described as a *settled tendency or usual manner of behavior* (9). God has given us a spirit of self-discipline, and as we mature in Christ, we can form healthy habits that pave the way for God's resounding presence in our life (Hebrews 5.14).

Third, do not FATIGUE. The enemy will not give up so easily. He is cunning, well-organized and good at hunting his prey. Like my dream, many times the attack of the wolf will come in many scenes. We must resist him until he finally gives up. Satan loves it when we get tired. Just like the wolf pack, he has great stamina and will stay on our trail for a while if he feels there is a chance we will grow weary.

When people are exhausted, they tend to make more mistakes, lose their resolve and want to give up. However, God promises that He will renew our strength. In fact, the Bible says we "will run and not grow weary" and "walk and not be faint" (Isaiah 40.31 NIV). God cannot lie (Titus 1.2). If the Bible promises something and our circumstances say otherwise, God will have to supernaturally provide. If we don't give up, He will give us supernatural energy, strength and stamina because He must be true to His Word.

These are the ways we stand firm, keep courage and renew our strength. However, when all else fails and we are at our wit's end, the Bible says that the name of *Jesus* is the most powerful name in all the world. In fact, just saying His name causes all heaven and earth to bow and declare that Jesus is Lord. Therefore, if we find ourselves faltering, we simply need to say aloud: "Jesus!" Satan knows he has no authority over Jesus, so we can begin to use our words to think and speak the name above all names, JESUS!

> "Therefore God exalted him to the highest place and gave him the name that is above every name, that at the name of Jesus every knee should bow, in heaven and on earth and under the earth, and every tongue acknowledge that Jesus Christ is Lord, to the glory of God the Father" (Philippians 2.9-11 NIV).

Winter of Doubt

Like stated earlier, the Grey Wolf doesn't fight fair. Wolves use the winter months to their advantage when hunting prey (12). By the time wolves decide to strike, their prey is hungry, tired and the thick snow around them steals their speed and strength. Spiritually, winter is an experience we must all go through. During this cold, barren season, we cling onto the promises and direction of God that we have already been given because our current situation is so bleak.

> "Do not turn to the right or the left; keep your foot from evil" (Proverbs 4.27 NIV).

When we are in a barren season, the Bible encourages us not to turn away from the course we are on by faith and to keep our feet from evil. What is the ultimate evil we are all prone to? This evil is the very reason why Jesus had to intervene. It is this evil that separates us from God and becomes a springboard for all other sins. This evil can be found in Isaiah 53, the Old Testament prophecy of our New Testament Jesus. It is the reason why Jesus had to take our sins on Himself.

> "We all, like sheep, have gone astray, each of us has turned to our own way; and the Lord has laid on him the iniquity of us all" (Isaiah 53.6 NIV).

The ultimate evil is to stop relying on Christ and to go our own way. During the winter months, it is very tempting to stop trusting God and His Word. Our circumstances seem to outright contradict God's promises in our lives, and we want to veer to the left or to the right. Once we change course without consulting the Lord, our feet have now stumbled into evil. Stepping outside of God's path is like telling Him that we no longer trust Him. Our circumstances are cold and bleak, and we think we can do a better job at making our way than God can.

Satan knows when we are enduring a time of winter, and he uses this season to his advantage. The circumstances around us seem lifeless and empty, and we are enduring a time of hardship, change or pain. Our doubt begins to build up like snowdrifts around us, and we sludge through the snow trying to cling onto the faith we once had. But true faith is not based on circumstantial evidence. Truth faith is based on belief alone.

> "Now faith is confidence in what we hope for and assurance about what we do not see" (Hebrews 11.1 NIV).

God wants us to have more faith in His Word than our situation. Faith is not rooted in physical sight of circumstance (2 Corinthians 5.7). Rather, it is rooted in God's Word found in the Bible and the promises God gives us through the work of the Holy Spirit. We were each created for a purpose, and the enemy wants to steal our destiny. Satan knows that if he can get us focused on our cold circumstances instead of God's faithfulness, we will lose ourselves in doubt. Once we wander into disbelief, we become more vulnerable to the attacks of the Grey Wolf.

Moreover, once we take our focus away from God and His Word, we can lose faith in ourselves. We begin to wonder if we heard God correctly. We start to question all the steps of faith we have taken so far. The enemy sees what God sees. He sees that we are victorious in Christ (1 John 5.4). He sees that we are a royal priesthood (1 Peter 2.9). He sees that we are coheirs with Christ (Romans 8.17). And Satan so badly does not want us to embrace our true identity because he knows he doesn't win, and he is a sore loser. He lost his beauty when he let pride sink into his heart, so he wants everyone to live out his condemned destiny.

> "Your heart [Satan] became proud on account of your beauty, and you corrupted your wisdom because of your splendor. So I threw you to the earth; I made a spectacle of you before kings" (Ezekiel 28.17 NIV).

Before we start listening to the lies of the enemy, we must remind ourselves that God sees truth. The devil sees lies. We can align our vision with God's vision because God's reality is true and eternal. It may feel weird at first, proclaiming who we are in Christ, but Jesus died to give us a new identity in Him. We disrespect and disregard Jesus' Finished Work on the Cross when we don't embrace that we are truly new creations in Christ.

> "Therefore, if anyone is in Christ, the new creation has come: The old has gone, the new is here" (2 Corinthians 5.17 NIV).

Furthermore, God has allowed us into the winter season as a gift. This gift is for us to produce true faith. Faith doesn't have to be big. It simply needs to be pure. The purest form of faith is one that is not based on circumstance but on His Word alone. We can produce this mustard seed of faith during the bleak winter months of our lives when all evidence contradicts God's Word. If we can cling onto belief even when the physical world around us screams otherwise, we will produce a pure drop of faith, and a little bit of faith goes a long way to dispersing doubt and making the impossible a reality.

> "He replied, 'Because you have so little faith. Truly I tell you, if you have faith as small as a mustard seed, you can say to this mountain, "Move from here to there," and it will move. Nothing will be impossible for you'" (Matthew 17.20 NIV).

Nothing is impossible with God, and He will strip down our situation to its bleakest point for us to produce a drop of faith that shows the whole universe that we believe Him more than anything else. God loves us no matter what. Nothing we do or don't do will change His mighty love for us. However, God is most pleased with us when we have faith. Faith only exists on earth. We won't need faith in heaven because we will be face-to-face with God's glory. Only in this temporal life do we have the chance to create and collect these precious gems of faith. And once we get into heaven, we can offer an armful of faith to God that we produced as we believed and trusted Him above all else.

> "And without faith it is impossible to please God, because anyone who comes to him must believe that he exists and that he rewards those who earnestly seek him" (Hebrews 11.6 NIV).

Finally, the best way to prepare for winter months is to get our gear ready. God does not leave us naked and vulnerable. He gives us everything we need to keep warm and strong during the dark, cold days. This gear is the Amor of God and it will help you stand firm during the winter seasons of life. God sees us as victorious warriors, which is why He has gifted us armor to stand strong and overcome the devil's strike on our lives.

> "Therefore put on the full armor of God, so that when the day of evil comes, you may be able to stand your ground, and after you have done everything, to stand. Stand firm then, with the **belt of truth** buckled around your waist, with

the **breastplate of righteousness** in place, and with your feet fitted with the readiness that comes from the **gospel of peace**. In addition to all this, take up the **shield of faith**, with which you can extinguish all the flaming arrows of the evil one. Take the **helmet of salvation** and the **sword of the Spirit**, which is the word of God" (Ephesians 6.13-17 NIV).

1. **Belt of Truth:** You are God's handiwork, and everything He creates is valuable and worthy.

   "For we are God's handiwork, created in Christ Jesus to do good works, which God prepared in advance for us to do" (Ephesians 2.10 NIV).

2. **Breastplate of Righteousness:** You have right-standing with God and have been reconciled back to Him through Christ.

49

"God made him who had no sin to be sin for us, so that in him we might become the righteousness of God" (2 Corinthians 5.21 NIV).

3. **Gospel Shoes of Peace:** Through Jesus, we have been given peace that is not based on our circumstances.

"Peace I leave with you; my peace I give you. I do not give to you as the world gives. Do not let your hearts be troubled and do not be afraid" (John 14.27 NIV).

4. **Shield of Faith:** We are shielded with God's supernatural and powerful protection by faith.

"Who through faith are shielded by God's power until the coming of the salvation that is ready to be revealed in the last time" (1 Peter 1.5 NIV).

5. **Helmet of Salvation:** We have the knowledge that no matter what

happens, God has saved us, and we will be with Him in heaven for eternity.

"To give his people the knowledge of salvation through the forgiveness of their sins, because of the tender mercy of our God, by which the rising sun will come to us from heaven" (Luke 1.77-78 NIV).

6. **Sword of the Spirit:** Out of all the armor, this is the only offensive weapon we've been given. The rest of the armor is for protection, but we fight back like Jesus did in the wilderness by using verses found in the Bible. Always keep God's Word by your side and ready.

   "Gird your sword on your side, you mighty one; clothe yourself with splendor and majesty" (Psalm 45.3 NIV).

Additionally, we should always pray! During those difficult seasons, our prayer time must be amplified. Since our circumstances are fighting against what we are believing for, we can continually go to God and let His Spirit warm, strengthen and satisfy us. Even in the most desperate places, God's love, goodness and favor can supernaturally pour into our situation. If our circumstances are hellish, we must bring heaven to us. When heaven touches down in our circumstances by faith, no evil—not even the Grey Wolf—can touch us.

> "And pray in the Spirit on all occasions with all kinds of prayers and requests. With this in mind, be alert and always keep on praying for all the Lord's people" (Ephesians 6.18 NIV).

Grey Wolf's Goal

We are not alone. Being spiritually attacked is not a sign of weakness or wrongdoing. In fact, Jesus was also spiritually attacked by the Grey Wolf. We can look at what happened in the wilderness after Jesus fasted for 40 days to get an up-close and personal account on the wolf's motives and tactics (10). Remember, Satan comes only to **steal, kill and destroy**, and he will deceive and lie to promote his agenda, and he bides his time until we are most vulnerable—alone, tired, fearful and wounded.

In Jesus' story, Satan didn't attack Jesus when he was in day 1 of his fast or day 10 or even day 20. The devil waited until Jesus had finished His 40-day fast before striking. Jesus was alone and starving in the wilderness. Satan loves to attack us during our time in the wilderness. The wilderness time is right after we receive our promise from God and before that promise comes to pass.

If it is a small promise, the wilderness time will be quick. However, if the promise is large, we can be in the wilderness for a long time—years and sometimes decades. Just before Jesus went into the wilderness to be tempted by Satan (Mathew 4.1), He was baptized by John the Baptist and the heavens opened up and God declared a promise to Jesus and the world: "This is my Son, whom I love; with him I am well pleased" (Matthew 3.17 NIV).

Finally, after years and years of waiting, the earth now has its promised Messiah, the Christ. God's Son among us to take the sins of the world.

> "He is the atoning sacrifice for our sins, and not only for ours but also for the sins of the whole world" (1 John 2.2 NIV).

Once Jesus received that promise from God, Satan took the opportunity to attack Jesus.

The devil does not want God's promise to Jesus to come to pass. Satan knows that the Son of God comes to "proclaim the good news," "bind up the brokenhearted," "proclaim freedom to the captives" and "release from darkness the prisoners" (Isaiah 61.1 NIV). Satan will do three things to prevent God's promise from coming to fruition. These three schemes of the enemy can also be applied to our own lives; so the next time we receive a promise from God, we can be ready.

First, Satan will tempt us to choose a lesser promise.

> "The tempter came to him and said, 'If you are the Son of God, tell these stones to become bread'" (Matthew 4.3 NIV).

Creating a meal may sound like a small deal, but when you are starving, it can be tempting to usurp the bigger promise for immediate gratification. Like I said earlier, walking in our God-given promises may take years. Plus, there will be many obstacles along the way. We have to keep our faith intact. We have to stand firm. And we have to be patient. Many times, it seems better to forget God's promise and just chase dreams that are easier to achieve. But those easier dreams don't take faith. And faith is the one thing that Jesus desires from us (Luke 18.8). We have to remember that though our promise seems impossible, with God all things are possible (Matthew 19.26).

Second, Satan will tempt us to abort the promise.

> "Then the devil took him to the holy city and had him stand on the highest point of the temple. 'If you are the Son of God,' he said. 'Throw yourself down for it is written: "He will command his angels concerning you, and they will lift you up in their hands, so that you will not strike your foot against a stone"'" (Matthew 4.5-6 NIV).

In essence, Satan tempted Jesus to commit suicide. Satan desires us to commit a similar suicide. This suicide could symbolize throwing our promise out the window. It could mean sabotaging our promise by our own actions of disbelief. However, it can also mean ending our own life. If the devil can't use us to achieve his evil plans, he would rather take us out of the picture altogether. Suicide is the 10th leading cause of death in the United States (11). Suicide is a very serious issue and a scheme that the enemy uses against us. When we are going through a dark season of being alone, tired, wounded and fearful, we become easy targets for this lie of the enemy. This is why being a part of a family in Christ is so important. We must aggressively seek to surround ourselves with people of faith during difficult times. Isolating ourselves is not an option.

> "If either of them falls down, one can help the other up. But pity anyone who falls and has no one to help them up" (Ecclesiastes 4.10 NIV).

Third, Satan will tempt us to take a selfish promise.

> "Again, the devil took him to a very high mountain and showed him all the kingdoms of the world and their splendor. 'All this I will give you,' he said, 'if you will bow down and worship me'" (Matthew 4.8-9 NIV).

Here is one of Satan's biggest lies. He deceives us into thinking our selfish desires only serve our self-interests, but they don't. There is good and evil, and there is no in-between. When we disobey God in order to chase our selfish desires, we are worshipping the evil one by doing his will and putting his agenda above God's. Many people think their actions are neutral, neither good nor evil. However, God created us to be vessels. Vessels are meant to be filled. If we are not filled with God's purposes, we will be filled with the enemy's plans. Vessels do not simply remain empty (2 Corinthians 4.7). Chasing God's promises may seem burdensome at times, but it is better to be on the right side of eternity, doing the will of God, not Satan.

"What good is it for someone to gain the whole world, yet forfeit their soul?" (Mark 8.36 NIV).

What did Jesus do to resist Satan's temptations? He used truth found in Scripture. Each time the devil tempted Jesus to choose a lesser promise, abort the promise or take a selfish promise, Jesus confronted the lie with truth.

1. **Choose the Lesser Promise:** "Jesus answered, 'It is written: Man shall not live on bread alone, but on every word that comes from the mouth of God'" (Matthew 4.4 NIV).

2. **Abort the Promise**: "Jesus answered him, 'It is also written: Do not put the Lord your God to test'" (Mathew 4.7 NIV).

3. **Take the Selfish Promise:** "Jesus said to him, 'Away from me, Satan! For it is written: Worship the Lord your God, and serve Him only'" (Mathew 4.10 NIV).

Satan also uses one more cunning tactic: He twists Scripture. When he tempted Jesus to throw Himself from the temple, he used verses out of context to justify his dare. He told Jesus that God would protect him. Yes, this assertion is true. Yet, Jesus knew that God's protection didn't give Him leniency to be reckless. We still must use common sense and obey the commands God has created as a safeguard for us. The Bible says that God will not give us more than we can handle; therefore, we should not add additional chaos to our lives by abusing His grace (1 Corinthians 10.13).

> "What shall we say, then? Shall we go on sinning so that grace may increase? By no means! We are those who have died to sin; how can we live in it any longer?" (Romans 6.1-2 NIV).

Finally, in my dream, the woman's foot was badly wounded by the Grey Wolf. Yes, thanks be to God that she got away; however, she will definitely need time to heal. Once we finally leave a spiritual attack and claim victory over the enemy, we need to allow ourselves a season to rest and heal. There will come a day that the time of trial will be a faint memory. We will be stronger and wiser. But until that day comes, we need to rest in the Lord. Here are some verses that we can speak over ourselves during our time of healing.

- "He heals the brokenhearted and binds up their wounds" (Psalm 147.3 NIV).

- "Come to me, all you who are weary and burdened, and I will give you rest. Take my yoke upon you and learn from me, for I am gentle and humble in heart, and you will find rest for your souls. For my yoke is easy and my burden is light" (Matthew 11.28-30 NIV).

- "But he was pierced for our transgressions, he was crushed for our iniquities; the punishment that

61

brought us peace was on him, and by his wounds we are healed" (Isaiah 53.5 NIV).

- "He will wipe every tear from their eyes. There will be no more death or mourning or crying or pain, for the old order of things has passed away" (Revelation 21.4 NIV).

- "'Go,' said Jesus, 'your faith has healed you.' Immediately he received his sight and followed Jesus along the road'" (Mark 10.52 NIV).

Now we know what to do when the wolf pack tries to prowl in our territory. First, we don't give Satan any roaming room by capturing every thought not of God and producing thoughts of God. The more truth-highways we create in our minds, the more the Holy Spirit can freely flow. Second, we stay in God's presence, in His Word and in His Church. The bigger our herd, the better.

Third, we stand firm, keep our courage and never give up. We use God's Word and other Christian resources to keep our faith strong and to rebuke the enemy's lies. We put on the full armor of God and wield our Sword, the Bible. We know that Satan wants only to steal, kill and destroy; but he has no authority over us. Our flesh has died in Christ and has been resurrected into eternity with God. We have God on our side, so we have nothing to fear. Nothing can snatch us out of God's mighty hands.

> "I give them eternal life, and they shall never perish; no one will snatch them out of my hand" (John 10.29 NIV).

Notes

1. James W. and Michal Ann Goll, Dream Language (PA: Destiny Image, 2006), pg. 237.
2. Biblegateway.com, "The Good Shepherd and His Sheep": John 10.1-20 NIV. https://www.biblegateway.com/passage/?search=john+10.1-20&version=NIV
3. Biblegateway.com, Prowling and Devouring Devil: 1 Peter 5.8-10 NIV. https://www.biblegateway.com/passage/?search=1+Peter+5%3A8-10&version=NIV
4. Biblegateway.com, Flesh and Spirit: 1 Corinthians 15.45-52 NIV. https://www.biblegateway.com/passage/?search=1+cor+15.45-52&version=NIV
5. Dr. Caroline Leafe in her book, *Switch on Your Brain*. Baker Books, 2013.
6. Sciencing: "How Do Wild Wolves Hunt in a Pack."

https://sciencing.com/do-wild-wolves-hunt-pack-8769011.html

7. National Geographic: "Wolf Hunting Tactics." https://www.youtube.com/watch?v=2jXxtQRy47A

8. BBC Earth, Frozen Planet: "Pack of Wolves Hunt a Bison." https://www.youtube.com/watch?v=8wl8ZxAaB2E

9. Marriam-Webster: Definition of Habit. https://www.merriam-webster.com/dictionary/habit

10. Biblegateway.com: Jesus Tested in the Wilderness. Matthew 4.1-11, https://www.biblegateway.com/passage/?search=Matthew%204%3A1-11&version=NIV

11. National Institute of Mental Health: www.nimh.nih.gov. https://www.nimh.nih.gov/health/statistics/suicide.shtml. If you are struggling with suicidal thoughts, call 1-800-273-TALK (8255).

12. Living with Wolves: "On the Hunt." https://www.livingwithwolves.org/how-wolves-hunt/

Meet Alisa

Alisa Hope Wagner writes words of inspiration and imagination. She's been married to her high school sweetheart for over twenty years, and together they raise their two sons and daughter in a Christ-centered home. She has a bachelor's degree in English and a master's degree in English Applied Linguistics. She has taught Bible studies, led discipleship small groups and lectured at churches, schools and universities.

Alisa is an international award-winning author of both fiction and non-fiction books.

She has been in two reality tv shows, competed and placed in bodybuilding competitions and won an MMA fight by TKO in a little over a minute. She is co-founder and editor of enLIVEn Devotionals that publishes award-winning anthologies that support world missions. She has written and published over thirty fiction and nonfiction books, which can be found her Amazon Page and Audible Page.